CW00517939

CHRISTIE WILLIAMSON has written poe
wandering the banks of Yell as a child
Courtney Hostel and as a Media (then Investments) student at the University
of Stirling. The poems in this collection began appearing in 2003, and pay
the big and the small questions in life their due. When performing as Federico
García Lorca in the Edinburgh Festival Fringe, 2006, Christie was invited to
create Shetlandic versions of some Lorca poems. These were succesful, and
resulted in his first publication – the pamphlet 'Arc o Möns' from Hansel
Co-operative Press, which won the Calum MacDonald Memorial Award
2010. His first book was *Oo an Feddirs*, published by Luath Press in 2014.

Since the publication of *Oo an Feddirs*, Christie's poetry has taken him all over
Britain and to the Americas and back. He always makes sure to leave poems
behind. He always comes back with more, the best of which are collected
here. He now invites you to walk with him through these *Doors tae Naewye*.

# Doors tae Naewye

CHRISTIE WILLIAMSON

**Luath** Press Limited
EDINBURGH
www.luath.co.uk

First published 2020

The publisher acknowledges receipt of the Scottish Government's Scots
Language Publication Grant towards this publication.

Scottish Government
Riaghaltas na h-Alba
gov.scot

ISBN: 978-1-913025-42-7

The paper used in this book is recyclable. It is made from low chlorine pulps
produced in a low energy, low emission manner from renewable forests.

Printed and bound by Bell & Bain Ltd., Glasgow

Typeset in 10.5 point Sabon by Lapiz

'*You will not be master of others or their slave.*'
JAMES JOYCE


'*Terrible old man!... sleeping in this gale, still thou steadfastly eyest thy purpose.*'
HERMAN MELVILLE

*for Sandy*

# Contents

*one of the dark places*

*of the earth*

*and this also*

Even dis nexus

        dis spun disc
            emorhc sid neve

     sweetened sylk spun

           haert

*even this nexus/this spun disc/even this chrome//sweetened silk spun//heart*

# Dawn

In LaGuardia I read
*The Silence of Men.*
My case is checked,
devices safe and close
to hand. I wait.

I see a guy – he could be anything
from forty to seventy-five. Dreads
hang loose around his neck.
This guy has lived.

I see the torn rags
that just keep his feet off the ground,
taking step after step, always
forward – to what?

I think of the heavy shoes
I paid those bastards at American
to carry. I want to dig them out, say
'Here you go buddy – walk a mile.'

Like all these dreams it slips
away as quickly as it came.
I sit, with ten kilos of books
and not one word to say.

# fish

Mother's Day, Kibble Palace

we fed wishes
to the carp
sharp shining coins
clasped between fingers

finally put
on what we wanted
thumbs veering upwards
like crocuses

stood in a row
we all let go
hopes glistening
under glass

you and I
sent treasure
falling
from the sky

before we opened
swimming eyes
saw Glasgow
flourish

# Original Features

Da sam pair o een, at shed mucus
an amniotic gunk sae mony year fae syne –
an whit dey irna seen at twinty fower frames o reference
an nae sikkind chance.

Sam pair o lugs, da iceberg organs
pickin up da vibes laek a Hammond
B3 in da spin tin tin o da black
an whicht an aathin in atween.

Sam neb fur whit's good fur me,
whit's no, whit's best left tae compost
doon an whit needs sookit up afore
hit geengs, turns or choost plen dries
awa ta nawtheen.

Sam gob, aa lips an teeth an tongue
as ready ta swalloo as it is ta spew
taestin da very truth o whit keeps
wis an whit speeds wis tae da deep
an bides hit's time ta say whit maun be sed.

A'm hed mair haircuts as a Argentinian
sovereign bondhowlder, seen fashions come
an geeng an style mature, cheenged haunds
intae keyboard curlin harbingers
o asset bubble self-inflicted trouble

at neddir man, baest nor god could hae
foreseen, preventit nor mitigaetit
ony mair as Noah could da flood
an I hae aa my original features,
da property o nae man, fur da profit

o aa at care ta keen, an keen
ta care. Dese are da parteecilars
ta be conveyed. Dese are at hom
in da cool, simmir breeze o richt noo.


*The same pair of eyes that shed mucus/and amniotic gunk so many years from now –/and what they haven't seen at twenty four frames of reference/and no second chance.//Same pair of ears, the iceberg organs/picking up the vibes like a Hammond/B3 in the spin tin tin of the black/and white and everything in between.//Same nose for what's good for me,/what's not, what's best left to compost/down and what needs sucked up before/it goes, turns or just plain dries/away to nothing.//Same mouth, all lips and teeth and tongue/as ready to swallow as it is to spew/tasting the very truth of what keeps/us and what speeds us to the deep/and bides it's time to say what must be said.//I've had more haircuts than an Argentinian/sovereign bondholder, seen fashions come/ and go and style mature, changed hands/into keyboard curling harbingers/of asset bubble self-inflicted trouble//that neither man, beast nor god could have/foreseen, prevented nor mitigated/any more than Noah could the flood/and I have all my original features,/the property of no man, for the profit//of all that care to know, and know/to care. These are the particulars/to be conveyed. These are at home/in the cool, summer breeze of right now.*

# Bitten

As subtle as a black eye
in a weddeen phawtoo
he surely kent fu ta whisper
i da lull o labour's release.

Da flysh trembles
atween her teeth.
Juice slidders aff her sylk
lips, dreeps sooth, sooth, sooth.

O boy, shø med him aaryt.
I'd laek ta see de dø ony better
pantless in Eden, i da shadoo

spreadin fae da wan tree
guid eneuch tae hoid da licht
fae da hale grund.

Even Gods can faa
cryin 'Whit's du don?'
at da sicht unseen o trust

dissolvin under fig laives
sendin gairdners
tae dir graves.

Wi angels at da grind
du'll keen du's closs
tae heevin whaur dir's fire.

Doon i da stoor, snaek een
bide dir time. Swallooin hale
da daily breid, he waets
fur feet tae dance him deid.


*As subtle as a black eye/in a wedding photo/he surely knew how to whisper/
in the lull of labour's release.//The flesh trembles/between her teeth. /Juice
slithers off her silk/lips, drips south, south, south./O boy, she made him
alright./I'd like to see you do any better/pantless in Eden, in the shadow//
spreading from the one tree/good enough to hide the light/from the whole
ground.//Even God's can fall/crying 'What have you done?'/at the sight
unseen of trust//dissolving under fig leaves/sending gardeners/to their
graves.//With angels at the gate/you'll know you're close/to heaven when
there's fire. //Down in the dust, snake eyes/bide their time. Swallowing
whole/the daily bread, he waits/for feet to dance him dead.*

# Rote

A split vote – a joke. To think we ever saw the road
twisting away to a nuclear free Argyll. It was always
going to take a while. Box as clever as you like,

there's always going to be some cheap tyke or other
paid handsome and well briefed fresh up from the corporate
campaign bus to spin a sweeter lie about why we're as well

just tholing the yoke a little longer. Honest folk like you
and I – what chance did we have of coming up trumps
against the lumpen uber trooper blue pinstripe eyeballing

the YES across your face and chest and aawhere else
in case anyone was plagued with any doubt.

Sweet sang the laevrick, high abön the Cuillin.
And if I lie deep and torn in the pull of the Minch, it is from there
I must rise.

# garnethill fox

did shø sink hir teeth
deep i da tiger's tail
feel hit's heft rage
ower da crest o da hill

or did shø kjiss hit
better oot, stripes airnt
lairnin lessons free
tae refuweegees near da end

o Rose Street choost afore
St Al's faas heevinwirds
fae da ruby two shoes
at danced dir wyes

roon cordon bustin jungles
hung laek hardback monochromes
aff an on, sangs risin
laek da kjist o a filskit city

at braithes de in
trow da sheen
an gleen o hir third
vulpine ee

*did she sink her teeth/deep in the tiger's tail/feel its heft rage/over the crest of the hill//or did she kiss it/better out, stripes earnt/learning lessons free/to refuweegees near the end//of Rose Street just before/St Al's falls heavenwards/from the ruby two shoes/that danced their ways//round cordon busting jungles/hung like hardback monochromes/off and on, songs rising/like the chest of an excited city/that breathes you in/through the shine/and glimmer of her third/vulpine eye*

# Flare

My love washed in
fae da tides o sin
at tugged da Atlantic wilds.
As wide as da wings
o da Albatross hit cost me
laek ony love can.

As deep as da geo
whaur I buried dat No
at rived da braeth fae me kjist
A'm haaled faurder in
as A'll ivvir win
afore I fin onythin oot.

As high as da cry
fae da first craw's nest
ta catch sicht
o da wastwird maas
is hoo faur A'll faa
trow da careless air
syne da waves
come tae cradle mi haert.

My love washed in
fae da tides o sin
an mi wirds
wis swept oot tae sea.
Syne du sails by da point
an ayont da last mead
dere du'll fin
whit remains o me.


*My love washed in/from the tides of sin/that tugged the Atlantic wilds./As
wide as the wings/of the Albatross it cost me/like only love can. //As deep
as the geo/where I buried that No/that ripped the breath from my chest/I'm
pulled further in/than I'll ever get/before I find anything out.//As high as the
cry/from the first crow's nest/to catch sight/of the westward gulls/is how far
I'll fall/through the careless air/before the waves/come to cradle my heart.//
My love washed in/from the tides of sin/and my words/were swept out to sea./
When you sail past the point/and beyond the last bearing/there you'll find/
what remains of me.*

# Dear

Here's a skin to begin to win on – taut
wi da tug o aathin du nivvir lairnt.

Here's a fraem ta hing a future on – nekkit
ta winds at blaa nae annsirs.

Here's a cushion ta faa, ta faa
ta watch rushin up at de time an agien.

Here's a blast at isna past hit.
Here's a winter warmin up.

Here's da rod tae da empty forest.
Here's da fitprints washd bi da sea.

*Here's a skin to begin to win on – taut/with the tug of everything you've ever learnt.//Here's a frame to hang a future on – naked/to winds that blow no answers.//Here's a cushion to fall, to fall/to watch rushing up at you time and again.//Here's a blast that isn't past it./Here's a winter warming up.//Here's the road to the empty forest./Here's the footprints washed by the sea.*

# Testament

after Killochries by Jim Carruth

Afore da wird, did da sharp solstice sun
burn da een ony less i da thrice iced
thrill o da bare Jül hill?

Wioot da book ta bind da willin
an da wance wanted fur mair
as da pooir o dir shoodirs, wha'd heed

da swalloo's promees o a lang nicht's wark?
Wha'd rise wi da sang o redemptive draems
still sweet i dir lugs ta pit brakkfist

on da table? Wha'd wakk da verges
o plooed an falloo fields? Wha'd fin
an mend da hols i da fence

whaar da wild wirld oot ower
could win in, whaar da saddled service
o a free man's haert could brakk oot?

*Before the word, did the sharp solstice sun/burn the eyes any less in the thrice iced/thrill of the bare midwinter hill?//Without the book to bind the willing/and the once wanted for more/than the power of their shoulders, who'd heed//the swallow's promise of a long night's work?/Who'd rise with the song of redemptive dreams/still sweet in their ears to put breakfast//on the table? Who'd walk the verges/of ploughed and fallow fields? Who'd find/and mend the holes in the fence//where the wild world out over/could get in, where the saddled service/of a free man's heart could break out?*

# Boxfu

for my perfect match

                                        Du stuck oot,
                                                hot heidit,
                                                        slender
boadied
                        ready fur da love struck
                                spark
                sheenin ower infinities
        settin lowe tae 'have ta be's
                                        gaein wye tae 'please
                pick me's.
                                        A'll no tell de ony lees
        whan I say 'Lass, du lat
                                my fire,'
                an nae mair whan I brakk da news
at hit still burns bricht
as suddern sea sylk sarks.
                                                Strike da not
                at ony du can raek athin
                                        dis scale du plays,
                aisy as a bairn's drum.

Sweet as honey

                                        comin hom.

*You stuck out,/hot headed,/slender/bodied/ready for the love struck/spark/shining over infinities/setting fire to 'have to be's/giving way to 'please/pick me's./I'll not tell you any lies/when I say 'Girl, you lit/my fire,'/and no more when I break the news/it still burns bright/as southern sea silk shirts.//Strike the note/that only you can reach within/this scale you play/easy as a child's drum.//Sweet as honey/coming home.*

# Ken Wast Yell?

Sound – tick – Yell tae da wastird
tides runnin laek da wirkins
o a clock at meezhirs mair
time as ee pair o lungs could respire.

Hoose lichts – tick – up fur da pilgrims
tae parade, awppin palms
touchin da cash box square
dan flicked aff fur da feature ta roll.

Print – tick – program decided
bi fair votes, practicalities
da package takkin pride o pliss
i da stentit Friday moarneen overland.

Sang – tick – Carla's ringin bittersweet
in hungry lugs afore da rods
dispersed wis tae da simmir dim
nesiks dancin tae da music o solidarity.


*Sound – tick – Yell to the westward/tides running like the workings/of a clock that measures more/time than one pair of lungs could respire.//House lights – tick – up for the pilgrims/to parade, open palms/touching the cash box square/ then flicked off for the feature to roll.//Print – tick – program decided/by fair votes, practicalities/the package taking pride of place/in the packed Friday morning overland.//Song – tick – Carla's ringing bittersweet/in hungry ears before the roads/dispersed us to the summer twilight/porpoises dancing to the music of solidarity.*

# Spark

Buckie bred an blyde
              tib   tiy   tseb  ad
              a tour de jour
    eence ta takk a skip
dnop dennob neerrih ad rewo
              an back in ees stride
                   ony gied an left
                       da keeper's feet glued
          etosoerc keal
          tae slippery girse
               markin da odds
               naw aa neewta
  an wan o a kind.

          An here's me, lucky eneoch
nac I tiwh nrial at
           keenin speereet, licht
           life
       isna lairnt.
       Hit's boarn.

*Buckie bred and happy/the best yet bit/of tour de jour/once to take a skip/over the herring boned pond/and back in his stride/only went and left the keeper's feet glued/like creosote/to slippery grass/marking the odds/between all one/ and one of a kind.//And here's me, lucky enough/to learn what I can/knowing spirit, light/life/isn't learnt./It's born.*

# Mainsails doon, masts asunder

Dey kent *l'inconnu de Limoise*
owerweel i da Dale o Waas
but here in big Islesburgh
dey wir nae pipes ta skirl. Hallelujah!

Fae aa aerts dey cam ta plick
an pluck dir fower dooble stringed
roond bellied, slender necked
bundles o musical joy.

Tuned laek a fiddle sans da owertones
o tortured cat at sent me howlin fur da hills
dey super-trouped aa da wye fae Greenland
mirriment tae douse Venetian harmonies

turned mi camino oscuro tae sole nostro.
Wha widna play dis haund until dir fingirs bled?
Birl da bus tae whitivvir mead du fancies – wave
da wand at canna help but faa anunder da spell
o da Shetland Mandolin Band.

*The knew the unknown of Limoise/perfectly well in the Dale of Walls/but here
in big Islesburgh/there were no pipes to skirl. Hallelujah!//From all compass
points they came to plick/and pluck they're four double stringed/round bellied,
slender necked/bundles of musical joy.//Tuned like a fiddle without the overtones/
of tortured cat that sent me howling for the hills/they super-trouped all the way
from Greenland/merriment to sweet Venetian harmonies//turned my dark path to
our sun./Who wouldn't play this hand until they're fingers bled?/Spin the bus to
whatever bearing you fancy – wave/the wand that can't help but fall beneath the
spell/of the Shetland Mandolin Band.*

# Meall

Du med a line i da saund
　　　　　whaur da white froosh
　　　　　　　　　o da spent waves
　　　　　sood nivvir cross.

Fur a time, dey kept dir pliss.
　　　　　Kept slippin back, sinkin
　　　　　　　　　doon trow grains
　　　　　o eence wis rock
　　battered sparklin
　　　　　bi lifetimes
　　　　　o leequeed saat.

But wha can keep da tides
　　in check? Wha can dø mair
　　　　　as geeng wi da flow,
　　　　　　　laek da pin sharp sun
　　　　　drappin intae aniddir spin
　　roond da bitten core
　　　　　　　　　o dy here an noo.


*You made a line in the sand/where the white froth/of the spent waves/should never cross.//For a time, they kept their place./Kept slipping back, sinking/ down through grains/of once was rock/battered sparkling/by lifetimes/of liquid salt.//But who can keep the tides/in check? Who can do more/than go with the flow,/like the pin sharp sun/dropping into another spin/round the bitten core/of your here and now.*

# Poor, becomin moaderit laetir

If I wis waddir I'd cheenge
i da blink o a untrained ee –

I'd be warm, laek da pert breists
o wid pigeons a smidgeon ower don,
a trifle gien

I'd be weet, laek monkfish cheeks
lattin da saat wash aff afore divin
back in tae aa dey keen

I'd be dull, laek a Wednesday nicht
Faesbuik timeline, wi nae single meme
o deservin wine

I'd be mawst mesel atween plaesis,
atween ee braeth comin in
an ee braeth gjaain oot

*If I was weather I'd change/in the blink of an untrained eye –//I'd be warm,
like the pert breasts/of wood pigeons a smidgeon over done,/ a trifle gone//I'd
be wet, like monkfish cheeks/letting the salt wash off before diving/back in to
all they know//I'd be dull, like a Wednesday night/Facebook timeline, with no
single meme/of deserving wine//I'd be most myself between places,/between one
breath coming in/and one breath going out*

# Firestarter

IM Scott Ward

                           He gied life
                      whaar he fan fuel,
haaled fae caald November skips,
               cut an dried fae mad livin trees
                    trivlin fur da lift
             or rived aff doors ta naewye
       keekit doon an oot.
Hit wis nivvir a mettir o if,
       ony fu hit cam tae licht,
                 cam ta be afore
           him
         wha sank,
            browt spark;
               cradled da rich laer
  i da catch o his braeth,
          gaffed aff rain at saffened
     da lick o flem
            at med wis rich,
   kent da dance
        widna be slockit.
                   Kent nawtheen lests
laek a fire
   set richt.

*He gave life/where he found fuel,/pulled from cold November skips,/cut and dried from mad living trees/groping for the sky/or ripped off doors to nowhere/kicked down and out./It was never a matter of if,/only how it came to light,/came to be before/him/who sank,/brought spark;/cradled the rich lore/in the catch of his breath,/laughed off rain that softened/the lick of flame/ that made us rich,/knew the dance/wouldn't be extinguished.//Knew nothing lasts/like a fire/set right.*

# Drap

A bowl o Angus straas
in June
.maerc iw
Whit hae dey
to dø
wi Tusla rakia
in September?
Dey dunna slink oot
o plastic bottlenecks
even if dey dø sit
an tempt da een
wi sunshine sookit doon,
slippit laek a mare
tae a love seek stallion.
Dey winna makk
da cloods o life
clear fae me thinkin,
eswol
midders mylk sweet clear sylk
ower da sair bons o mi confusion,
mi doot an free mi tongue
tae fin wirds at laive shadows
bricht as dry taing fires
i da sober moarneen.
An yit, dir sumtheen
aboot da saft explosion
at fills me moo,
da elevation
o dis corporeal
barrafu o memories
lost laek flysh

                              aff a weel baettid waek
                              line
                      at minds me o braethin
                  simmir trow mi lips
              o aa da aedges saftnin
                      tae a waarm pool
          giein de troot eftir troot
                  toort ritfe
                              til aa da bellies at ivvir
                              mettired

              is kjettled fu
  o keenin du

                      haes da wit
                                      o a thoosand
                                      owld yows,

          da strent o a ox
                  on steroids
                                              an da
                                              speereet
      o da sweetest fruit
                                  ivvir ta faa

          an rot awa.

A bowl of Angus strawberries/in June/with cream./What have they/to do/with
Tusla Rakia/in September?/They don't slink out/of plastic bottlenecks/even if
they do sit/and tempt the eyes/with sunshine sucked down,/slipped like a mare/
to a lovesick stallion./They won't make/the clouds of life/clear from my thinking/
loosen/mothers milk sweet clear silk/over the sore bones of my confusion,/my
doubt and free my tongue/to find words that leave shadows/bright as dry seaweed
fires/in the sober morning./And yet, there's something/about the soft explosion/
that fills my mouth,/the elevation/of this corporeal/barrowful of memories/
lost like flesh/off a well baited weak line/that reminds me of breathing/summer
through my lips/of all the edges softening/to a warm pool/giving you trout after
trout/after trout/until all the bellies that ever mattered/are tickled full/of knowing
you/have the wisdom/of a thousand old ewes,/the strength of an ox/on steroids/
and the spirit/of the sweetest fruit/ever to fall/and rot away.

*has been*

Sookit sair dry
      dis washt oot
            streetchd weelkim
gnarts nöba boba
     airmed empty saftly saftlies
          o silt an clay
              eence kent choost whit
            needed doin.


*Sucked sore dry/this washed out/stretched welcome/floating above strong/
armed softly softlies/of silt and clay/once knew just what/needed doing.*

# In da first pliss...

to mark the Golden Wedding Anniversary of Rex and Sandra Doyle

Dey say at life's a marathon
            no a sprint,
                    but if du's nivvir raced
                            da wind
                ta fling dy airms
                                    roond music
tae dy haert
            du'll nivvir
                        win hom
                                tae taest simmir sun
                                        sokk de
                    in hir sweet
                sylk
    kjiss.

                            Dey say at love's a
                                    journey
                no a destination
but if du's nivvir
watched a roulette baa
        rushin roond rid, black,
                    rid, black
                        ta faa atil da ony slot
        du biggit aa
                dy aathin on
                                du's nivvir taestit gold,
nivvir brokk da taep
                    ta turn an see

                                        du'd dø
                                           hit ower agien.

Had da haund at slippit
              dat plain band apö dy fingir
                           as dear tae de as life,
                                      as dreamin
         as precious as da lifetime
       riot o diamonds
rived fae stoor
              fur which hit staunds.


*They say that life's a marathon/not a sprint,/but if you've never raced the
wind/to fling your arms/round music/to your heart/you'll never/get home/
to taste summer sun/soak you/in her sweet/silk/kiss.//They say that love's a/
journey/not a destination/but if you've never/watched a roulette ball/rushing
round red, black,/red, black/to fall into the only slot/you built all/your
everything on/you've never tasted gold,/never broke the tape/to turn and see/
you'd do/it over again.//Hold the hand that slipped/that plain band onto your
finger/as dear to you as life, /as dreaming/as precious as the lifetime/riot of
diamonds/ripped from dust/for which it stands.*

# A peerie bit lost

Wi dis feet first birse
fae da deil du keens
tae onythin could happen.

A peerie bit fun
whan dat bruck at's strewn
dy flair starts ta win

intae da bin, an du begins
ta fin a wye
fae aa ower da plaes

tae bein da best
du kin be da day.
A peerie bit no fun

an dan da habits
fecht hit oot.
Wha's side is du on?

Will du lat da good
or da ill eens win? Lat dem fin
dir wye aneath dy skin

intae dy inner spin?


*With this feet first squeeze/from the devil you know/to anything could
happen.//A little bit fun/when the rubbish that's strewn/your floor starts to
get//into the bin, and you begin/to find a way/from all over the place//to being
the best/you can be today./A little bit no fun//and then the habits/fight it out./
Whose side are you on?//Will you let the good/or the bad ones win? Let them
find/their way beneath your skin//into your inner spin?*

# Green

No, I won't. I can't possibly accept that.
I am *not* the colour showing around the gills
of that *Salmo Salar*. Were it only to swim.
What a difference we'd see. But the stream
is torrid down there where the sharp rocks
break it white for the time of its short leap
back into running away to sea.

And as far as my resemblance to *brassica oleracea*
goes, that is entirely in your own head.
It simply does not bear any sort of scrutiny.
If anything, I'm more like the *Corylus avellana,*
trying, trying my best to grow. Burning
in the dark of the night.

# Unkan Genesis

In da beginneen
                dey wir a darkness
      big eneoch an dark
          eneoch ta burst a hol
        i da koll bucket
    haalin waarmth
             in fae da caald.
                An da darkness covered
aa da things
    at wis, an aa da things
      at wisna
        i da heevins abön
          an da grund
            sunken i da sook o hit's tide.
                  Dan,
          dey wir a spark o licht
        at wis bön hoidin
   waetin fur da exack
      richt time
        ta brakk da monotony
      o da notheenniss
at wis aathin afore hit.
Da mirk saa da licht
    an da mirk
        hed not a clue           whit ta dø
        aboot dis brilliant bairn
          laundit apö his shores.
            Dat wis day wan, an fae dan
             da mirk haesna riggit
                ee hail day yit.

                    Fur aa dat,
                  he's gien naewye.
                He's gjaain naewye.
              He's bidin his eternity,
            da best,
          maest brilliant dark
        du ivvir saa.


*In the beginning/there was a darkness/big enough and dark/enough to burst
a hole/in the coal bucket/pulling warmth/in from the cold./And the darkness
covered/all the things/that were, and all the things/that weren't/in the heavens
above/and the ground/sunken in the suck of its tide./Then,/there was a
spark of light/that had been hiding/waiting for the exact/right time/to break
the monotony/of the nothingness/that was everything before it./The gloom
saw the light/and the gloom/had not a clue what to do/about this brilliant
child/landed upon his shores./That was day one, and from then/the gloom
hasn't dressed/one whole day yet./For all that/he's gone nowhere./He's going
nowhere./He's biding his eternity,/the best,/most brilliant dark/you ever saw.*

# Case

The embodiment of siecle
removed for exhibition.
Mother of pearl –
fancy.
Fruit wood
wouldn't you?

Perspective chatters
through silence, imperfect
true as granite.
Ink smudged thumbprints
rest on black foam.

Open the doors,
lock yourself in.
When the lids are closed
the spirit is freed.

# Pulling the scissors out

Whan hit comes tae da crunch
neddir dem nor de is half as sharp
as du'd hae wis aa believe.

Doon yundroo i da black pit, du'll no
hae faur ta geeng ta fin shite,
winna win in an oot wioot a scar

ta shaa fur de troubles. Whan hit comes
tae da crunch, metal bends an roosts –
edges an points geeng wi time. Ony wounds

can heal wi prime time bills fittin hols
fillin sjøn at winna wakk aniddir mile.
On da surface o da wattir fitprints folloo

eftir da storm. Dir plenty mair fysh
on da iddir side, bellies rived awppin
tae da saat an smokk at keeps dem,

plenty tae gie syne da flysh stops
sweein wi da sweet sharp speereet
o a clean slaet, me an de waetin
fur da crunch.

*When it comes to the crunch/neither them nor you is half as sharp/as you'd have us all believe.//Down there in the black pit, you'll not/have far to go to find shite,/won't get in and out without a scar//to show for your troubles. When it comes/to the crunch, metal bends and rusts –/edges and points go with time. Only wounds//can heal with prime time bills fitting holes/filling shoes that won't walk another mile./On the surface of the water footprints follow//after the storm. There's plenty more fish/on the other side, bellies ripped open/to the salt and smoke that keeps them,//plenty to give once the flesh stops/stinging with the sweet sharp spirit/of a clean slate, you and me waiting/for the crunch.*

# Harbour

Traffic free, da waa
howlds ticht, horses
dancin whicht oot ower.

Chained fast
tae solid grund
cabin kyissed craft

bobbed i da saef wattir,
gunwales bumpin
an squashin boo

intae boo. Ayont
da strip o concrete
an ston mortared tagiddir

da winds whip
da sea sair
an wild

lash eftir lash
tuggin roond a blind ee
at keeps lookin

nivvir fins a wye in
tae da noost,
tae da lee
we howld een aniddir in.

*Traffic free, the wall/holds tight, horses/dancing white out over.//Chained fast/
to solid ground/cabin kissed craft//bobbed in the safe water,/gunwales bumping/
and squashing bow//into bow. Beyond/the strip of concrete/and stone mortared
together//the winds whip/the sea sore/and wild//lash after lash/tugging round a
blind eye/that keeps looking//never finds a way in/to the safe haven,/to the lee/we
hold one another in.*

# Manhattan

for JBK and the dream team, Midtown East

In Lexington Avenue, I felt
no pain, the cherries full
of Big Apple Juice were loose
and easy on the lazy Saturday.

Standing clear
of the looking glass
the class rose to salute
the coming fall.

So close. But as ever
you know the same old story.
I missed more than home
as the ticket burned

a hole the factor fifty
could never plug.
Beneath the grid, a failure
lurked around the cornerless

circle, roamed up and down
the town's extended play – no
country home, the time zoning
out as the tracks disappear

into airways thickening up nicely
thank you very much, the sunshine
promising delivery by close – the day
just and no more reaching out

for alarmed fingertips
to sleep through.

# Halfwye Hoose

Neddir clossir as du maun be
      nor faurdir awa as du'd laek
dir nae rod iddir as da een
      du haes at dy feet.

Takk de braeth at da tap
      lat da hale straett afore de
grip dy tyres laek oo
      tae heddir.

Bide as lang as da haal
      o da haundline birls oot
an under an du leans in
      an da wirld leans in wi de.

Naebody wan onywye
      ithoot passin da Halfwye Hoose.
Naeby gied by hit
      ithoot lookin.

*Neither closer than you must be/nor further away than you'd like/there's no road other than the one/you have at your feet.//Take your breath at the top/ let the whole straight before you/grip your tyres like wool/to heather.//Stay as long as the haul/of the handline spins out/and under and you lean in/and the world leans in with you.//Nobody got anywhere/without passing the Halfway House./Nobody went past it/without looking.*

# Into the wormhole

In loving memory, Alexander Hutchison
'*Thy word is a lamp unto my feet, and a light unto my path*'

Where do we come from?
From the vast stretches of darkness
which shine as bright as a cold cut cluster
of diamonds, as warm as a child's embrace.

Where are we going?
Beyond the sparkle which blinds us
to the fear of knowing there is a fire that burns
without feeding, a clean sheet on which to rest safe
from the vagaries of misspent breath.

Why are we here?
To find the answers
don't matter so much as the way
we hear the questions, to be free from the need
to be right which traps our song before
the angels can hear it.

What is it all for?
For watching the diaphragm
of the galaxies relax; for sharing all we have
with all we have; for holding close to our chests
as the soft warmth of the clay opens beneath our feet.

# Bound

*for Campbell*

Wance da lightnin struck thrice
I kent da time wis richt
ta slip da rop aff da grind, stride
up da girse, takk da style
wi ony panache I could muster
an pick mi wye alang da dark path.

Ahint coortins draan quick tae thunder
a future moored tae da truth heard
da rain but nivvir felt da winds
trow ticht waas risin fae da side
o a green hill.

Faur awa fae Ladysmith, da boat dips
a nose intae da bielin sea. Da bridge
is fu, da hull stappit. Da final teddir
tae da laund is slippit.

Sheenin unhindered i da nicht
comes da holy spray, sokkin aathin;
da dowtir as pure as a baitless heuk;
da midder o invention, as necessary
as da braeth du takks whan da storm
is passed.

*Once the lightning struck thrice/I knew the time was right/to slip the rope
off the gate, stride/up the grass, take the style/with any panache I could
muster/and pick my way along the dark path.//Behind curtains drawn quick
to thunder/a future moored to the truth heard/the rain but never felt the
winds/through tight walls rising from the side/of a green hill.//Far away from*

*Ladysmith, the boat dips/a nose into the boiling sea. The bridge/is full, the hull stuffed. The final tether/to the land is released.//Shining unhindered in the night/comes the holy spray, soaking everything;/the daughter as pure as a baitless hook;/the mother of invention, as necessary/as the breath you take when the storm/has passed.*

# A telling

My daughter is the truth. On Sunday mornings
she runs through from her slumber, holds me
in her warmth before I wake. On schooldays
she snores through half a dozen alarms, cowers
from the light I direct from bulb or burning sun.

My daughter is the truth. She is crawling down
a barely shoulder width gap with a screwdriver
to whack the tails off blast frozen salmon
so the trolleys can roll out and I can pack them
fast by the boxload and wheel them to the freezers
before they begin to thaw out again.

My daughter is the truth. She hurts her knee
finding out how roller skates work and keeps
straight on going, smart to the way they slide
in her chase towards mastery in summer sun.

My daughter is the truth. She is the flesh
of a girl half her age evaporating in Hiroshima
so a roomful of men in suits can feel better
about themselves for a few moments
before the glory fades.

My daughter is the truth. She is crunching
through knee deep snow to build a carrot
nosed pal for the day with your wellied
feet fighting numbness and the frost
nipping your cheeks and nose as red
as a May Day parade at the Kremlin.

My daughter is the truth. She is the drying
ink at the bottom of the printed first tab
of an Excel workbook explaining exactly
how the water supply of an African country
is going to make a handful of faceless
individuals even richer and by when.

My daughter is the truth. She is unannounced,
unexpected, not always what you think you want
and mostly what you need.

My daughter is the truth. She is a raggle taggle
dreadlocked gaggle of nothing to losers locking
down the latest back room deal and running
their own lives despite the best efforts
of everyone invested in the same old game
of brown paper envelopes never being pushed
too far.

My daughter is the truth. Can I open my heart
a little further to her? Let me try. Can I build
a world fit for her to grow into? For that, my friends,
I need your help.

# Core

    Fae flysh

               cam flysh

        an dere i da haert

              o Swiss bank rich fruit

                      new laives

              is turned ower

fu o sap green promise.

                 Fur aa dey look

                    laek mulch i da grund

     dey sook life fae sphere

       tae sphere

                   til aathin kent

                   an aathin uncan

      is wan.

          Feel da juice                 dreep doon.

Taest da loss                   o sookin fruit

                at canna be picked.

*From flesh/came flesh/and there in the heart/of Swiss bank rich fruit/new leaves/are turned over/full of sap green promise. /For all they look/like mulch in the ground/they suck life from sphere/to sphere/until everything known/ and everything unknown/are one./Feel the juice drip down. /Taste the loss of sucking fruit/that can't be picked.*

# St Cyrus

Tiny feet trippin

ower safe saunds

I had da shøn

socks tucked in

an folloo.

Dir nane as blinn

as him at winna see,

nane sae deef

as hir at plugs

lugs

lang lost

tae da music

o da hurried tide.

Da thistle

spikes a rekird simmir

as weet feet

steer cloods

o golden stoor

intae chilled

wattirs.

Bleached wid benkles,

swelters in Caesar strang

ultra pacific doses, skimped

an saved up

fur a fond

*au revoir.*

*Tiny feet tripping/over safe sands/I hold the shoes/socks tucked in/and follow//*
*There's no one as blind/as he that won't see/no one as deaf/as she that plugs/*
*ears/long lost/to the music/of the hurried tide.//The thistle/spikes a record*
*summer/as wet feet/steer clouds/of golden dust/into chilled waters.//Bleached*
*wood bends/swelters in Caesar strang/ultra pacific doses, skimped/and saved up/*
*for a fond/au revoir.*

# Catch

Siller dances apö da sun
free flowin laek a risin
tide fat wi mackerel

frish laek da drift
hurlin Nort Atlantik
chills an fugs skywards.

Sauchiehall Street nivvir saa
sic a exotic flock o birds
as caaed an cooried on da Foula cliffs.

Ilka line ivvir slippit
maun hae lures an bait an huiks.
Some bait is taestier as iddirs.
Some huiks nivvir laive your moo.

Here's aniddir catch
ta haal ahsore. Wast o dis
lies ony gold.


*Silver dances upon the sun/free flowing like a rising/tide fat with mackerel//
fresh like the drift/hurling North Atlantic/chills and fogs skywards.//
Sauchiehall Street never saw/such an exotic flock of birds/that squawked and
sheltered on the Foula cliffs.//Every line ever dropped/must have lures and
baits and hooks./Some bait is tastier than others./Some hooks never leave
your mouth.//Here's another catch/to haul ashore. West of this/lies only gold.*

# Traveller

*for AD*

He left behind a stone
green seam shining
between grit grey days

what sea did it swim
free from in times
forgotten?

Who did it bribe
to hide beneath
the near sky?

Above Balmaha
the clouds burn
hot, uneven

my jacket
softens the bite
of fire

by the water's edge
I weigh ballast
to steer me straight.

# Bird

Aa flap, nae fecht. Sae first
glance wid gie. But plenty
arroos haes dookit anunder dat
seeminly total sketch.

Syne da beak bobbed back up
abön da wattir, da sprayed
mist aff da dryin wings
sank intae underfit

even da herdist kaes wid windir
'Sall I crack, faesd wi dis
unbidden sentinel?'
Nae mön
ivvir shon
sae fu as da cry
fleein fae da thrapple
tae da gluffed air shø'd circled

squarin up tae laund
locked een jumpin oot
o sockets, böts bielin fur grund
nivvir high eneoch ta jink free
o da deadly, tooirin boo primed
predominant afore de. Aa fecht. Nae flap.

*All flap, no fight. So first/glance would give. But plenty/arrows have ducked
beneath that/seemingly total sketch.//When the beak bobbed back up/above the
water, the sprayed/mist off the drying wings/sank into underfoot//even the hardest
case would wonder/'Shall I crack, faced with this/uninvited sentinel?'/No moon/
ever shone/as full as the cry/flying from the throat/to the startled air she'd circled//
squaring up to land/locked eyes jumping out/of sockets, boots boiling for ground/
never high enough to jink free/of the deadly, towering bow primed/predominant
before you. All fight. No flap.*

# Held fast

ta celebrate fifty year o Magnie an Eunice
In da bleak mid winter

                                    a union.

And at the going down of the sun

                                  a beginneen.

     Yay, though I am fearfully

                an winderfully med

               I do

                  and

                    ton od I

   choost whit I choose

                  and

     ton esoohc I tihw
    an I choose mairryin

                     pid feirb ad i

  atween Jul an Ne'erde;
I choose sharin

            whittivir bed haes med hit's wye

                 fur wis ta lie in

    .sdeh yraew riw tser na

                I choose no tae waandir
                fae dy side;

   I choose no ta pit
    a sowl afore de.
I choose bein wi de ay
   eespeeshilly whan wir iddirwise
   poseeshinned on da globe.

                 I choose seein aa dy flaas
                .med ruf ed nivol na
        I choose believin at we can baith
    .riddina nee sa gnarw sa eb

I choose believin at dat gies wis

ycnerruc ron latipac ridden

ower een aniddir

but gies wis

een aniddir

ithoot which aa wi hae

means notheen.

But hits no whit we choose at makks wis

.siw sesoohc tihw s'tih

A sang

shineth in the darkness,

and the darkness

comprehendeth it not.

ssijk A

to rest, remain and abide with you,

Amen.

*In the bleak mid-winter/a union./And at the going down of the sun/a beginning./Yea, though I am fearfully/and wonderfully made/I do/and/I do not/ just what I choose/and/what I choose not/and I choose marrying/in the brief dip/between Christmas and New Year;/I choose sharing/whatever bed has made its way/for us to lie in//and rest our weary heads./I choose not to wander/from your side;/I choose not to put/a soul before you./I choose always being with you/especially when we're otherwise/positioned on the globe./I choose seeing all your flaws/and loving you for them./I choose believing that we can both/ be as wrong as one another./I choose believing that gives us/neither capital nor currency/over one another/but gives us/one another/without which all we have/ means nothing./But it's not what we choose that makes us/it's what chooses us./A song/shineth in the darkness, and the darkness/comprehendeth it not./A kiss/to rest, remain and abide with you,/Amen.*

Ivvir haal a muckle ston
      fae hit's plug?
    ycatsce ad ees rivvI
   o dank boond scurriers urgent
    oot o da raek
        o da sun, see dem
    scamper sooth, ta fin whit?
        ered med skkat tihW
      afore aa iddir?
        Da company?
        Da maet?
    Or da quality
      ?tchil ad o

*Ever pull a big stone/from its plug?/Ever see the ecstasy/of dank bound
scurriers urgent/out of the reach/of the sun, see them/scamper south, to find
what?/What takes them there/before all else?/The company?/The food?/Or the
quality/of the light?*

*one of the dark places*

# Utterance

*'In the beginning was the word...'* John 1:1

I da bloodied birse o hawkin life
        fae da nawtheen at da haert
             o een an aa, dey wir soond
    fae lips at sookit oot
  ivviry last drap
        o risen agenn.
               Sood sense be med
         o ony birlinn baas o licht
    ayont wir raek
  hit slips itae da mirk
      syne we loss da link
        tae da in/oot brute beauty
    o frish air i wir trotts
da agonies an ecstasies
            o zero tae wan
  an aa da wye back
      ta makk a black hol
        ta sing wir mysteries doon,
    as fluid an fearfu as da haet draft o air
    liftin da eagle
      ayont wir sicht.

*In the bloodied squeeze of digging life/from the nothing at the heart/of one and all, there was sound/from lips that sucked out/every last drop/of risen again./Should sense be made/of any spinning balls of light/beyond our reach/it slips into the gloom/when we lose the link/to the in-out brute beauty/of fresh air in our throats/the agonies and ecstasies/of zero to one/and all the way back/to make a black hole/to sing our mysteries down,/as fluid and fearful as the hot draft of air/lifting the eagle/beyond our sight.*

# Tree

Underneath the canopy
snowdrops break the ice
trembling
in the slow creep
of sunshine.

Hacked back branches
reveal a track
we pass one deep
free to follow
where open hands
and hearts have hewn.

It takes more than broken
heaters and crumbling
concrete to kill
the right idea
should it grow
in the right mind.

Come, bite the apple
fallen far from bliss.
The bark
of the unbroken cross
carries more
than a shadow
of menace.

# Recline

Eftir da mysteries
o da Bon Accord Grill
wis bön weel an truly
digested, nae navigation

wid be complete less a bellyfu
o St Clair air, aa da wye fae A deck
tae bolted portholes.
As broadcasts fizzed an foondird

wi da starnwird soup
atween wis an Bressay
ony celluloid guaranteed da murder
o hunders o meenits.

Da scale o da sea we pitched apö
wis onythin but minor. Aa at sank
wis da ivories dat nicht, but under
synthetic duvet waves

music draemed o howldin a ocean
in hir airms. Da dance o da moarn's
brakkfist bell wis waetin aff da harbour,
da captain's voice in tune wi da surf
kyissin aniddir day tae life.


*After the mysteries/of the Bon Accord Grill/had been well and truly/digested,
no navigation//would be complete without a bellyful/of St Clair air, all the
way from A deck/to bolted portholes./As broadcasts fizzed and foundered//
with the sternward soup/between us and Bressay/only celluloid guaranteed*

*the murder/of hundreds of minutes.//The scale of the sea we pitched upon/ was anything but minor. All that sank/was the ivories that night, but under/ synthetic duvet waves//music dreamed of holding an ocean/in her arms. The dance of tomorrow's/breakfast bell was waiting off the harbour,/the captain's voice in tune with the surf/kissing another day into life.*

# Place

You'll tell me it's a disgrace. You'll be right.
But whatever whatever textbook you think
you might have read will say the thing about
normal distributions is they are anything but.

Where you do find them, they're all well and good
for the busy, grumbling middle. On the way up
you must admit things are nothing if not steep.
Hard going. A sair fecht.

Racing down the other side, where we're told
we should all be aiming, isn't always as comfortable
as you might think – seeing sharp rocks racing up
calling to the grumbling, busy middle
'What happened to you?'

Why not just take the whole pile
and fling them down the stairs?
The madness method is often best – mean
though it may seem to the average bear.

# St Catherine's

Coated optics
conservatory

Da hills o Clift
watch oot

Doon by da fit
o da galloos hill

takk dy braeth
awa


*Coated optics/conservatory//The hills of Clift/watch out//Down by the foot/of the gallows hill//take your breath/away*

# Growth

If du'd a delled da grund, pickit oot
da cuttins choost richt fur da spot
an wattird an fed an pruned an spokkin up
da bush aa by dy sel, wha could blaem de
fur grabbin on wi baith haunds
haalin hit closs tae dy kjist, an plantin
a muckle, weet Yis kjiss on da lips o cheenge.
I dunna hae ta tell de fu hit swees,
canna pit wirds tae da döl o de hale bein
bein rived, canna keen fu lang de scars'll bide.
My dear freen, keep growin. Hae patience.
An mind, da presence o thorns da day
doesna mean da absence
o roses da moarn.

*If you'd have dug the ground, picked out/the cuttings just right for the spot/ and watered and fed and pruned and spoken up/the bush all by yourself, who would blame you/for grabbing on with both hands/pulling it close to your chest, and planting/a big, wet Yes kiss on the lips of change./I don't have to tell you how it stings,/can't put words to the sorrow of your entire being/ being torn, can't know how long the scars will stay./My dear friend, keep growing. Have patience./And remember, the presence of thorns today/doesn't mean the absence/of roses tomorrow.*

# Meeting Demand

burking, n – to murder, as by suffocation, so as to leave no or few
marks of violence

No getting out of it now the trapdoor's
blue beneath your feet, chained to their fate
kicking at the odds. A burking's too good for you.
The Grassmarket ghouls are harem scarem
there to see the dance between nothing
and infinity gasp again. On the slab
your belly enlightens us, the only evidence
coming kings will take from you.
Time to snap out of it. Your once
unseen hands are tight behind your back.

The medics keep the cut they need.
Now you reap what you stitched up
out of no one missing the crop.
The only grave you ever dug was your own.
Who now shall make head nor tail
of your anatomy of greed?

# No Rush

Hush      hush hush hush
                there's no  rush
                              hsur hsur   hsur
       the factory gate
                    never came today;
           the crowds of late
     appointment keepers
               are nowhere to be seen.
                         The only
                                 thing that's
                               bigger
                         than the everyman
                         out here
              is the sea that sucks
                      ni levarg eht
                         the gravel out
         through sky high tides'
                teeth.
                    Sun blinds kites calm.
There's no rush
           hsur hsur hsur
     nowing the
     hush      hush   hush      hush

# Villainy

Is dir nae good end tae dis adventure in sicht?
Is daeth da noblest offerin in wir gift tae gie?
Fu can we takk dis darkness an turn hit intae licht?

Da grice gobble at da trough aa day, aa nicht.
Dir nae a day geengs by some species doesna dee.
Is dir nae good end tae dis adventure in sicht?

Agin centuries o victories giein aa da wirld dir richts
da dugs o war is barkin, an barin blüd bricht teeth.
Fu can we takk dis darkness an turn hit intae licht?

Da cliff is comin at wis as fast as Messerschmitts
an clingin tae da wheel is füls choost prayin we can flee.
Is dir nae good end tae dis adventure in sicht?

Will Prince Regents an Presidents someday realise wi a fricht
dir come agin a power wi which dey canna cut a deal?
Fu can we takk dis darkness an turn hit intae licht?

Brokkin an battered though wir draems micht
be, tagiddir wir minds is med up ta be set free.
Dis is da good end tae wir adventures trow da nicht.
Noo we takk dis darkness an turn hit intae licht.

*Is there no good end to this adventure in sight?/Is death the noblest offering in our gift to give?/How can we take this darkness and turn it into light?// The pigs gobble at the trough all day, all night./There's not a day goes by some species doesn't die./Is there no good end to this adventure in sight?//Against centuries of victories giving all the world their rights/the dogs of war are barking, and baring blood bright teeth./How can we take this darkness and turn it into light?//The cliff is coming at us as fast as Messerschmitts/and clinging to the wheel are fools just praying we can fly./*

*Is there no good end to this adventure in sight?//Will Prince Regents and Presidents someday realise with a fright/they've come against a power with which they cannot cut a deal?/How can we take this darkness and turn it into light?//Broken and battered though our dreams might/be, together our minds are made up to be set free./This is the good end to our adventures through the night./Now we take this darkness and turn it into light.*

# Loom

Knit wan, purl awa
athin da ribs fur mair
as du ivvir lippened.

Da needles click clackin
dir wye trow da hammer
stirrup an anvil

man smith a bled
ta skin bricht Tygers
a million times ower.

Invertabrate, du'd bend
fur ony wind, bow
tae ony wave at cared

ta slap agin da brokkin
shalls cast bi generations
o spoots an buckies.

Hit's no choost hips
at hop aboard
bandwagons careenin

fur dir haedmist stint
i da yaird afore dir boarn
anew i da fug, unspottable.

Fae da tips o dy taes
tae dy croon, du's royal
as a lon stag, wild

abön da splatch o cotton
rich bogs, watchin, waetin
fur de ta sink in.


*Knit one, purl away/inside your ribs for more/than you ever expected.//The
needles click clacking/their way through the hammer,/stirrup and anvil//must
smith a blade/to skin bright Tygers/a million times over.//Invertebrate, you'd
bend/for any wind, bow/to any wave that cared//to slap against the broken/
shells cast by generations/of razor clams and buckies.//It's not just hips/
that hop aboard/bandwagons careening//for the final stint/in the yard before
they're born/anew in the fog, unspottable.//From the tips of your toes/to your
crown, you're royal/as a lone stag, wild//above the splatch of cotton/rich bogs,
watching, waiting/for you to sink in.*

# Keep your head up, keep kicking, don't drown

So your KPIs have slipped below your basic SLA again
and that nice chat we had doesn't seem to have done
the dirty dick, so you see, these hands of mine are tied today,
you've left me with no choice but to implement
a KYA, with the possible escalation without immediate results
to a MYLAFM. Make no mistake, my boy I'm watching you
like a hungry hawk with a new prescription who's eating
for half a dozen. In other words, the bizzo will continue
working to support your absolute commitment at a Mind
Body Soul kind of level to saving my comfortably proportioned
posterior. Don't say we don't spare a thought for posterity.
As you know, our input to credit and credit like decisions
is widely sought, and you my boy have long since kissed goodbye
to your AAA days. What's more, my innumerate fag from the best
days of my life is running this country's economy, so you get
to bow before the ground I walk on, until your vertebrae link up
at least, but for now it's time for me to do the talking
and you to put one foot in front of the other, so get your arse out
of my sight and get back to your work and don't make me speak
to you like that again because whatever you might think
I don't like it, does no good for my little problems, and we've both
got far better things to do with our time than listen to me
opening my mouth and letting my hungry guts rumble.

# Bounty

for Hazel, 10.3.13

At da end o da sea
        dir a rocky shore
                kjettled bi purple
        an yalloo tongues
o sun.
              I da simmir,
                  du can dip
              de taes
      i da warm kjiss
    o da Atlantic, an hae grains
        o grund granite
            polish dy feet clean.
                        Even here, A'm no
                        halfwye
                            tae haddin da
                            eternal truth
                at blossomed
            in dy belly;
        da magic, da mystery
      da implausibility
            spun laek sylk
                        ivviry day
        bi de.

*At the end of the sea/there's a rocky shore/tickled by purple/and yellow tongues/of sun.//In the summer,/you can dip/your toes/in the warm kiss/of the Atlantic, and have grains/of ground granite/polish your feet clean.//Even here, I'm not halfway/to holding the eternal truth/that blossomed/in your belly;/the magic, the mystery/the implausibility/spun like silk/every day/by you.*

# Diego

Da black key stuck. Da door
tae mair as du can keen
whit ta dø wi twined music
tae pointless fingirs, tae lugs

dug in fur winter, rum drunk
bi dennir time, aa barrels
birlinn tae read da score.
Twall blocks sooth o sense

dir time ta takk da hale
flair under wings slow
tae awppin, no closin in ony
kind o hurry. Dir nae

class da day, nae dreels tae bore
intae da polished wid. Choost ent
an whan du lippens nawtheen
da hammer 'll strike, unlock
whit wir bön growin tagiddir.


*The black key stuck. The door/to more than we can know/what to do with
twined music/to pointless fingers, to ears//dug in for winter, rum drunk/
by lunch time, all barrels/spinning to read the score./Twelve blocks south
of sense//there's time to take the whole/floor under wings slow/to open, not
closing in any/kind of hurry. There's no//class today, no drills to bore/into
the polished wood. Just listen/and when you expect nothing/the hammer will
strike, unlock/what we've been growing together.*

# Forgetting how to pray

Doesna hae tae be fur ay.
Da deep end's gien naewye

an drier lips as dine
haes intoned tae da divine.

Choost bekis hit slipped dy mind
doesna mean dir ony less or mair

oot dere as ivvir wis. Here. Noo.
Aa hit takks. Aa du haes.

Naebody's gjaain ta listen
if du winna.


*Doesn't have to be forever./The deep end's gone nowhere//and drier lips than yours/have intoned to the divine.//Just because it slipped your mind/doesn't mean there's any less or more//out there as ever was. Here. Now./All it takes. All you have.//Nobody's going to listen/if you won't.*

# Fine Times

Lower Hillhead, Lerwick
circa 1992. I fin da Good
Sodger Šjvejk. Aa trow dat grim
Shaetlan winter I stamped
around Europe wi his waett
i mi bag. Hit lightened da rod.

Byres Rod, 2018 an owld comrade
grips mi haund. He teaches me
tae fin Tony Blair's *A Journey*
an relocate da tome fae Famous
Lives tae True Crime. He snugs
soondly in wi his ain kind.

Crichton's Close, 2003 afore a crood
sublime an ridiculous, I fin
whit hit means tae hae lugs
tuned in tae da exposed wirkins
o mi mind. Tucked amang da shelves
I fin as mony paths awppin as I dare.

*Lower Hillhead, Lerwick/circa 1992. I find the Good/Soldier Šjvejk. All through that grim/Shetland winter I stamped/around Europe with his weight/in my bag. It lightened the road.//Byres Road, 2018 an old comrade/grips my hand. He teaches me/to find Tony Blair's* A Journey */and relocate the tome from Famous/Lives to True Crime. He snugs/soundly in with his own kind.// Crichton's Close, 2003 before a crowd/sublime and ridiculous, I find/what it means to have ears/tuned in to the exposed workings/of my mind. Tucked among the shelves/I find as many paths open as I dare.*

# Winging it

Da shadoo cast bi crosses
               sessorc na deirriak
    slippit tae roch grund
riapersid a ni em naf

                  laek a Christmas tree
                  psirc ad rewo nireddils
             catarct o a loch

                       yppat yppit denrut
                  bi a legendary run fae da sun.

                       ruahw eaf esor llihc A
               mi haert sood a bön
                          ni nirednilg litnu
                                  tae da low sun I saa

                    kcifrep yd o oodahs ad
                  pair o white wings
                        ria ad sserac
                  choost abön da slice
                  nidnuats rittaw o

        still atween wir graesfully
htaena rittaw ad ,stsierb nidilg
                  bielin wi da eager paddles

                            meews mednat a o
                    necks stuck oot
                            fur better

                ruaw ruf
                  fur ay

*The shadow cast by crosses/carried and crosses/slipped to rough ground/
found me in a disrepair//like a Christmas tree/slithering over the crisp/cataract
of a loch/turned tippy tappy/by a legendary run from the sun.//A chill rose
from where/my heart should have been/until squinting in/to the low sun I
saw//the shadow of your perfect/pair of white wings/caress the air/just above
the slice/of water standing//still between our gracefully/gliding breasts, the
water beneath/boiling with the eager paddles/of a tandem swim/necks stuck
out/for better/for worse/forever*

# Fare

Now that all of the ways have been found
and all of the paths have been followed round
what's left to wither into the ground?
What shoots for the Easter sun?

Here where the wind from the Firth of Clyde
blows snide in the face of human worth
who can ignore the music of hope?
Who can search the shore for more
than the crush of concrete tides?

This is the body of life
broken for time to reclaim.

This is the blood of a dying god
shed that the skin may grow whole again.

# Gone Midnight

Wha'll saat da waves? Da eens at crash
white wi da gluff o rocks puncturin
da lumbar o da flott atween low wattir
an high wi dir sokkit, serrated imperviability?
Da eens at tongue saft intae shingle an pebbles,
intae samphire marshes pricklin green i da fu mön?

Wha'll slip a nip o sumtheen sharp tae da tides,
pit hairs on dir kjist an gie dem sumtheen
tae schow wi? Wha'll snib da padlocks
an oge back in tae lat creamy heid
eftir creamy heid settle atil da saft
gapin belly o da deep?

Shaa me a man at can feel da spray o milennia sokkin
fae his taes tae his croon wioot faain ta bruck
ivvry laandin or twa an a'll shaa de a net at dips in
an oot, at fills an spills an haals alang da boddom o whit lies
aneath da very keel we feel we maun ay bide abön.

Da Clyde swees sair at Cappielow as aniddir cup run
grinds tae a halt. Even noo, whan aa da pages is turned
an da ink's run dry as dust sood du slip da lid aff da well
an drap dy can as faur as du maun he'll yield yit
fae deep i da haert o things dat still cowld truth.

*Who'll salt the waves? The ones that crash/white with the fright of rocks
puncturing/the lumbar of the float between low water/and high with their
saturated, serrated imperviability?/The ones that tongue soft into shingles
and pebbles,/into samphire marshes prickling green in the full moon?//
Who'll slip a nip of something sharp to the tides, put hairs on their chest
and give them something/to chew with? Who'll snib the padlocks/and creep*

*back in to let creamy head/after creamy head settle into the soft/gaping belly*
*of the deep?//Show me a man that can feel the spray of millennia soaking/*
*from his toes to his crown without falling apart/every landing or two and*
*I'll show you a net that dips in/and out, that fills and spills and drags along*
*the bottom of what lies/beneath the very keel we feel we must all stay*
*above.//The Clyde stings sore at Cappielow as another cup run/grinds to a*
*halt. Even now, when all the pages are turned/and the ink's run dry as dust*
*should you slip the lid off the well/and drop your can as far as you must it'll*
*yield yet/from deep in the heart of things that still cold truth.*

Da brithliss trott
            ad i deraor
                pitch nicht
                    teew, tfas o
        sweet deid hippo maet sun.
Is dis
        da end
                    o da aert?

Is          dis          wis?


*The breathless throat/roared in the/pitch night/of soft, wet/sweet dead hippo*
*meat sun.//Is this/the end/of the earth?//Is this us?*

*of the earth*

# Acknowledgements

Poems included in this collection have appeared in the following magazines and anthologies to whose editors I am grateful – *Fourfold*, *The New Shetlander*, *Northwords Now*, *Honest Error*, *Gutter*, *The Café Review*, *Causeway/Caibhsir*, *Laldy*, *the Poets' Republic*, *My Time*, *Writing into Art*, *Scotia Extremis*, *New Boots and Pantisocracies*, *Better Than Starbucks* and *Campus*.

For support and guidance on poems and poetry specific and general, I am grateful amongst many others to Christine De Luca, Stewart Alexander Sanderson, Jeanette Lynes, Jim Ferguson, Roseanne Watt and Michael Symmons Roberts.

I also owe gratitude and more to Al Filreis, Anna Strong and everyone at the Kelly Writers House in Philadelphia for the paradise of poetry they offer freely and openly to all who care to find it.

For maintaining my cultural buoyancy, I am grateful to the Scottish Poetry Library, St Mungo's Mirrorball and the Clydebuilt community, StAnza, the Scottish Writers Centre and the Granada class of 2018.

My thanks also go to Creative Scotland without whose support key elements of this volume would remain void.

I am very grateful also to my publishers, Luath Press for the great work they continue to do publishing well written books worth reading.

Thanks also go to all the far flung Williamsons for the horizons they've opened for me over the years, and most of all to Oliver, to Verity and to Hazel without whom these pages would indeed be empty in every sense of the word.

# Some other books published by **LUATH PRESS**

## Oo an Feddirs

Christie Williamson

ISBN: 9781910021620 PBK £8.99

*Oo an Feddirs* is the first full collection from established poet Christie Williamson. It carries the striking imagery and rhythm which came through 'Arc o Möns', Williamson's translation of poems by Federico García Lorca, to themes of family, love and loss. Not so much a manifesto as a manifestation through poetry of what it's like to be him – a living, breathing human being like any other.

A striking collection of over 70 poems, some of which have been published in magazines as diverse as *New Shetlander*, *Poetry Scotland*, *Northwords Now*, *Gutter* and *New Writing Scotland*. 'Parasites' was shortlisted for the Wigtown Poetry Competition in 2006.

## Scotia Extremis

### Poems from the Extremes of Scotland's Psyche

Brian Johnstone and Andy Jackson (eds.)

ISBN: 9781912147564 PBK £9.99

*Scotia Extremis* brings together a gallimaufry of poets to take a sideways look at what makes – and makes up – Scotland by examining the country's 'icons'. Featuring specially commissioned works by the National Makar Jackie Kay, plus acclaimed poets including Robert Crawford, Imtiaz Dharker, Douglass Dunn, Vicki Feaver, John Glenday and almost 100 more, all are tasked with probing extremes.

Each brace of contrasting poems tackles the extremities of the nation's culture by looking obliquely at 'icons' at opposite poles to each other. From Laphroaig versus Buckfast, to Oor Wullie against Black Bob, to Jimmy Shand meeting Jack Bruce, and Cullen Skink taking on Irn-Bru, these vivid and varied poems bring to life the people, places and motifs that form the complex and contradictory soul of Scotland.

## Scotia Nova

### Poems for the Early Days of a Better Nation

Tessa Ransford and Alistair Findlay (eds.)

ISBN: 9781910021729 PBK £7.99

Scotland's Independence Referendum on 18 September 2014 resounded with claims from all sides that a better Scotland is not only possible but necessary, whether remaining with the Union or leaving it. Scotland's artists and writers have long cultivated a distinct and independent cultural tradition undimmed – indeed frequently provoked – by political union. The project remains unfinished as the country heads towards totally unprecedented territory. The only sure thing seems to be that the political status quo is not an option, the only question being the extent of the changes ahead.

# **Luath** Press Limited

*committed to publishing well written books worth reading*

LUATH PRESS takes its name from Robert Burns, whose little collie
Luath (*Gael.*, swift or nimble) tripped up Jean Armour at a wedding
and gave him the chance to speak to the woman who was to be his wife
and the abiding love of his life. Burns called one of the 'Twa Dogs'
Luath after Cuchullin's hunting dog in Ossian's *Fingal*.
Luath Press was established in 1981 in the heart of
Burns country, and is now based a few steps up
the road from Burns' first lodgings on
Edinburgh's Royal Mile. Luath offers you
distinctive writing with a hint of
unexpected pleasures.
Most bookshops in the UK, the US, Canada,
Australia, New Zealand and parts of Europe,
either carry our books in stock or can order them
for you. To order direct from us, please send a £sterling
cheque, postal order, international money order or your
credit card details (number, address of cardholder and
expiry date) to us at the address below. Please add post
and packing as follows: UK – £1.00 per delivery address;
overseas surface mail – £2.50 per delivery address; overseas airmail –
£3.50 for the first book to each delivery address, plus £1.00 for each
additional book by airmail to the same address. If your order is a gift,
we will happily enclose your card or message at no extra charge.

**Luath** Press Limited
543/2 Castlehill
The Royal Mile
Edinburgh EH1 2ND
Scotland
Telephone: +44 (0)131 225 4326 (24 hours)
email: sales@luath. co.uk
Website: www. luath.co.uk